A BLUE BANNER
BIOGRAPHY

Mariah Carey

Kathleen Tracy

P.O. Box 196
Hockessin, Delaware 19707
Visit us on the web: www.mitchelllane.com
Comments? email us: mitchelllane@mitchelllane.com

Mitchell Lane PUBLISHERS

Copyright © 2007 by Mitchell Lane Publishers. All rights reserved. No part of this book may be reproduced without written permission from the publisher. Printed and bound in the United States of America.

Printing		2	3	4	5	6	7	8	9

Blue Banner Biographies

Alan Jackson	Alicia Keys	Allen Iverson
Ashanti	Ashlee Simpson	Ashton Kutcher
Avril Lavigne	Bernie Mac	Beyoncé
Bow Wow	Britney Spears	Carrie Underwood
Christina Aguilera	Christopher Paul Curtis	Clay Aiken
Condoleezza Rice	Daniel Radcliffe	Derek Jeter
Eminem	Eve	50-Cent
Gwen Stefani	Ice Cube	Jamie Foxx
Ja Rule	Jay-Z	Jennifer Lopez
J.K. Rowling	Jodie Foster	Justin Berfield
Kate Hudson	Kelly Clarkson	Kenny Chesney
Lance Armstrong	Lindsay Lohan	**Mariah Carey**
Mario	Mary-Kate and Ashley Olsen	Melissa Gilbert
Michael Jackson	Miguel Tejada	Missy Elliott
Nelly	Orlando Bloom	P. Diddy
Peyton Manning	Paris Hilton	Queen Latifah
Ritchie Valens	Rita Williams-Garcia	Ron Howard
Rudy Giuliani	Sally Field	Selena
Shirley Temple	Tim McGraw	Usher

Library of Congress Cataloging-in-Publication Data
Tracy, Kathleen.
   Mariah Carey / by Kathleen Tracy.
      p. cm. — (Blue banner biographies)
   Includes discography (p.), bibliographical references (p.), and index.
   ISBN 1-58415-516-7 (library bound : alk. paper)
   1. Carey, Mariah—Juvenile literature. 2. Singers—United States—Biography—Juvenile literature.
I. Title. II. Series: Blue banner biography.
ML3930.C257T73 2007
782.42164092—dc22
[B]
            2006014807

ISBN-10: 1-58415-516-7   ISBN-13: 9781584155164

ABOUT THE AUTHOR: Kathleen Tracy has been a journalist for over twenty years. Her writing has been featured in magazines including *The Toronto Star*'s "Star Week," *A Biography* magazine, *KidScreen* and *TV Times*. She is also the author of numerous biographies, including *William Hewlett: Pioneer of the Computer Age* and *The Fall of the Berlin Wall, Justin Berfield, Lindsay Lohan*, and *Kelly Clarkson* for Mitchell Lane Publishers.

PHOTO CREDITS: Cover—Peter Kramer/Getty Images; p. 4—Photog/Ipol/Globe Photos; pp. 7, 23—Kevin Mazur/WireImage; p. 9—Supplied by Alpha/Globe Photos; p. 12—Barry King/ WireImage; pp. 15, 16—Getty Images; p. 20—Jonathan Green/Globe Photos; p. 18—Steve Granitz/ WireImage; p. 26—Associated Press, AP; p. 28—Kevin Winter/Getty Images.

PUBLISHER'S NOTE: The following story has been thoroughly researched, and to the best of our knowledge represents a true story. While every possible effort has been made to ensure accuracy, the publisher will not assume liability for damages caused by inaccuracies in the data and makes no warranty on the accuracy of the information contained herein. This story has not been authorized or endorsed by Mariah Carey.

CONTENTS

In 2001, Mariah Carey worked to finish the sound track for Glitter, a movie based loosely on her own life. The pressure began taking its toll. Between stress, promoting the film, and staying up all night long recording, Mariah crashed and ended up hospitalized for exhaustion.

Breakdown

*E*ven though she had sold more records than any other female recording artist ever, Mariah Carey still felt she had something to prove in the summer of 2001. After years of planning, she had finally filmed *Glitter*, a movie loosely based on her life. In the film, Mariah plays an aspiring young singer who becomes a star with the help of a DJ, and she falls in love with him. Now the real-life Mariah was working around the clock to get the sound track finished for the film's August premiere. In between recording sessions, she would run out and do publicity to promote the movie.

During an interview with MTV, she admitted she was running on fumes. "It's an insane time in my life. It's crazy. Everything is going on like really fast. . . . We're trying really hard to make this deadline and just really get everything together. I'm honestly really, really delirious and stressed out and overworked and doing too much. I haven't slept in, like, two weeks." She said that if she wasn't so busy, she'd "be crying on the floor, OK? But it's also an amazing time in my life because it's a fresh new happy situation."

The sound track was Carey's first album for her new label, Virgin Records, which had signed her to a staggering $80 million contract—four albums with a guarantee of $20 million apiece. The pressure to prove she was worth the money was intense, she admitted in *Allure*, especially since her first single for the label, "Loverboy," had barely made a blip on the music charts. "Right now I've just signed this big deal that everybody's watching. I don't have time to relax."

As the summer wore on, it became increasingly clear that Mariah was pushing herself too hard.

As the summer wore on, it became increasingly clear that Mariah was pushing herself too hard. The stress worsened as the early buzz on the movie was not positive. In late July, she posted a troubling message on her official web site, telling her fans, "I don't know what's going on with life . . . I just want you to know that I'm trying to understand things . . . right now, and so I really don't feel that I should be doing music right now."

Another message read, "What I'd like to do is just a take a little break or at least get one night of sleep without someone popping up about a video. All I really want is to just be me and that's what I should have done in the first place. . . . I don't say this much but guess what? I don't take care of myself."

Mariah signs her "Loverboy" single from her album Glitter. *The single was not very popular.*

Soon, it wouldn't be a choice.

On the evening of July 25, 2001, Carey's mother made a frantic call to 911. The New York *Daily News* reported that earlier in the day, in a fit of frustration, Mariah had smashed some plates and glasses, cutting herself in the process. She had remained emotionally distraught throughout the day, prompting her mother to finally call for medical help.

Carey was taken to a New York–area hospital that night, and then transferred to an undisclosed facility and put under psychiatric care. Her publicist released a statement saying the singer had been hospitalized for emotional and physical exhaustion. In other words, she had suffered a breakdown.

While the public was shocked, those close to her weren't. "It wasn't a shock at all," producer Jimmy Jam told MTV. "I think Mariah is a person that burns the whole candle. In our short time working together . . . she not only works really, really hard but works on many, many things at the same time."

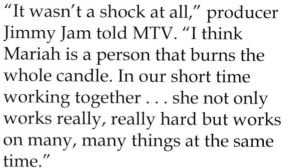

Few people noticed Glitter was in record stores on September 11, 2001—the day terrorists attacked the World Trade Center and the Pentagon.

Mariah was discharged from the hospital two weeks later, and the label pushed back the release of her new album by three weeks, from August 21 to September 11. But few people even noticed that *Glitter* was in record stores on September 11, 2001 — the day terrorists attacked the World Trade Center and the Pentagon. Any hopes for a boost from the movie were quickly dashed. At media screenings, critics openly laughed and were no kinder in their reviews. *Village Voice* reviewer Michael Atkinson wrote that when Carey "tries for an emotion — any emotion — she looks as if she's lost her car keys." Christy Lemire of the Associated Press called the movie "a preposterous, poorly written love letter to herself."

The *Glitter* album fared little better. It would become the worst selling record of Carey's career. Around the same time, her three-year relationship with singer Luis Miguel

Mariah began a three-year relationship with Latin heartthrob Luis Miguel in 1998. When the relationship ended in 2001, Carey denied media reports that her physical breakdown was due to distress over Miguel. She said the breakup was mutual.

fizzled out. In January 2002, Virgin cut its losses and dropped Carey from the label, buying out her contract for $28 million. Later that same year, Carey's father died.

The lesson Mariah would learn from this dark period was simple: What doesn't kill you will simply make you stronger.

Taunted

No matter how rich Mariah Carey is today, the memories of growing up poor remain fresh and vivid in her mind, as does the pain of growing up an outcast.

Mariah Angela Carey was born March 27, 1970, in Huntington, New York, located on Long Island. Her mother, Patricia Hickey, was of Irish descent. Her father, Alfred Roy Carey — who had been born in Venezuela — was African-American and Hispanic. Mariah's brother, Morgan, and sister, Alison, were ten and nine years old, respectively, when Mariah was born.

When Patricia and Alfred, an aeronautical engineer, got married in 1960, Patricia's family was upset that she was marrying a black man. The response from the couple's neighbors was no better. "They went through some very hard times before I was born," Mariah told *People*. "They had their dogs poisoned, their cars set on fire and blown up. It put a strain on their relationship. There was always this tension. They just fought all the time."

When Mariah was three years old, her parents divorced. Alison went to live with Alfred, who eventually moved to Washington, D.C., while Mariah and Morgan stayed with their mother. Hickey, a professional opera singer who performed as a soloist with the New York City Opera in the late 1960s and early 1970s, says her daughter was born with a musical gift.

Hickey was rehearsing a song from Verdi's *Rigoletto* and missed a cue. "But Mariah didn't," she told writer Steve Dougherty. "She sang it — in Italian — at exactly the right point. She wasn't even yet three.

"From the time Mariah was a tiny girl, she sang on true pitch; she was able to hear sound and duplicate it exactly."

Hickey eventually gave up her singing career to work as a full-time vocal coach. However, she didn't always have enough students to make ends meet. With money often scarce, she and her children moved thirteen times. One of Mariah's earliest memories was riding in her mom's car, which Patricia called the Dodge Dent. "I was looking out the window at the supermarkets and people driving normal cars and I was like, *When I grow up, I want to not have a Dodge Dent*," she told Rory Evans. "I want to evolve from this. But more than that, I wanted to express myself through music, because that was what made me happiest."

Carey says that when she was four, she would sneak the kitchen radio into her bedroom so that she could sing along

> **"From the time Mariah was a tiny girl, she sang on true pitch; she was able to hear sound and duplicate it exactly."**

After their parents divorced, Mariah and her brother, Morgan, pictured here, stayed with their mother. Carey's sister, Alison, went to live with their father, who eventually moved to Washington, D.C. The baby of the family, Mariah was ten years younger than Morgan and nine years younger than Alison, so growing up it was mostly just Mariah and her mother struggling to get by.

to the songs. That love of music created a special bond between Mariah and her mother.

"That is such a major part of both our lives," Mariah says. "My father is more of a cerebral person. He's a great mathematician, an aeronautical engineer, and he's completely opposite of me in terms of what he excels at. I'm horrible at math. We don't have the same interests." Even though they didn't have that much in common, Mariah said in *Ebony* that she has "good memories of doing things with him when I was a little girl."

Some of her fondest memories were meeting her father's large family. "I wish I had been a part of it more. I loved them when I met them. I'd never experienced a big family like that, because my mother's family basically disowned her when she married my father."

Although Mariah never suffered the violent racism her parents endured, being biracial made her an outcast. She didn't fit in with either white or black kids she met. "It's hard growing up like that. But lucky for me, my mother . . . always taught me to believe in myself, to love all the things I am. In that sense I'm very lucky, because I could have been a very screwed up person."

By the time she was in second grade, Mariah knew her voice was special. She was also certain she would be a famous singer one day.

"Because my mom did it for a living when I was young, I knew it could be more than a pipe dream," she said in the *New York Times*. "My mom always told me, *You are special. You have a talent.* She gave me the belief that I could do this."

To prepare, Mariah sang in the choir and began writing songs while attending Oldfield Middle School. As she got older, she focused all her energy on making it as a singer, determined not to end up like her mother.

". . . lucky for me, my mother . . . always taught me to believe in myself, to love all the things I am."

"I always looked at her . . . and thought she could have gone really far, but she gave it up. I think that motivated me even more. She gave me that sense that when it's time, you have to go for it."

Mariah wasted very little time making her childhood dreams a reality.

A Star Is Born

With her mother's encouragement, Mariah started looking for work as a singer while she was attending Harborfields High School. At first, she did background vocals at various Long Island recording studios. Then for her sixteenth birthday, her brother, Morgan, paid for her to have a professional demo tape made.

After that, Mariah began to travel regularly to Manhattan, trying to break into the music business. Many times she wouldn't get home until the middle of the night, then she'd have to drag herself to school the next day. Ironically, Carey never told any of her friends about her aspirations, preferring it to be her secret.

She told *Blender* magazine she would even intentionally sing off-key at school because it gave her confidence knowing, "I have this secret . . . this gift; this thing I know they can't do. You just wait."

Shortly after graduation, Mariah moved to Manhattan, sharing a modest, sparsely furnished apartment with two

Mariah signs autographs to promote her album Mariah Carey. *The album would make her a superstar.*

friends. Her bed was a mattress on the floor. As a career backup, she attended beauty school and supported herself working a series of jobs, including coat checker and waitress. She would later admit to being fired from at least twenty restaurants because of her attitude. Carey told *Ebony* she lasted only one day at a beauty salon where her job was to sweep up hair. She quit after the owner insisted that she use the cutesy name Echo.

She spent most of her first year in New York writing songs and recording demo tapes that showed off her four-and-a-half-octave range. The following year, a friend told her that Brenda K. Starr, known for recording dance songs, was looking for backup singers and convinced Mariah to audition. Starr, impressed, hired Carey to sing background vocals on a number of recordings. She would also become one of Mariah's staunchest supporters.

When Brenda saw Tommy Mottola, chairman of CBS Records, at a music industry party in 1988, she hauled Mariah over and made her introduce herself. Mottola took Mariah's demo tape and later, on the way home, listened to it in his car. He was so impressed that he turned around and went back to the party to find Mariah. She had already left.

Mottola spent the next week tracking Carey down. When he finally found her, he offered her a contract. After

After hearing her demo tape, record executive Tommy Mottola signed Carey to her first record deal. Her debut album, Mariah Carey, *sold over 6 million copies and earned Carey her first Grammys — for Best New Artist and Best Pop Vocal Performance.*

less than a year in New York, Mariah had a record deal. Her first album, *Mariah Carey*, was released in June 1990 and would sell over six million copies. She won two 1991 Grammys—for Best New Artist and Best Pop Vocal Performance for "Vision of Love." Mariah was officially the latest "overnight" music sensation.

Still, she bristled in a *New York Times* interview when it was suggested she hadn't paid her dues the way most performers do before singing success.

"I condensed 10 years of work into three," she pointed out. "It was like fast-forwarding. I worked around the clock. I would waitress until midnight, then go to the studio and work till seven in the morning on the album, then sleep, then do the whole thing again, day after day. No one helped me out, and I lived on very little money."

Just a year and a half later, in September 1991, Carey released her second album, *Emotions*. Normally, there's at least a two-year wait between albums, but Carey was eager to show more of her artistic range.

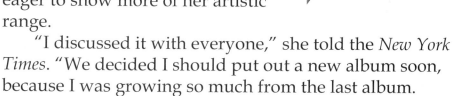

"I condensed 10 years of work into three. It was like fast-forwarding. I worked around the clock."

"I discussed it with everyone," she told the *New York Times*. "We decided I should put out a new album soon, because I was growing so much from the last album.

"I also wanted to use the influences of all the music I loved, like Motown stuff and Stevie Wonder. I felt the up-tempo songs were a little over-produced on the first record."

Mariah plays to the crowd in Los Angeles as she opens her U.S. tour in 2000.

If it seemed Mariah had an unusual amount of creative control for a relative newcomer, there was a reason. Although Mottola was twenty years older than Carey, and he was married, the two had become romantically involved. Not only was he Carey's professional mentor, he was her boyfriend as well. Eventually, Mottola left his wife and married Carey.

To many it seemed as if Mariah was living out a real-life Cinderella fairy tale. But she and Mottola would not live happily ever after.

Fractured Fairy Tale

*C*arey and Mottola were married on June 5, 1993, in Manhattan. The bride wore a $25,000 gown designed by Vera Wang that had a 27-foot-long train—which took the help of six people to stuff into the limo for the ride to the church. The couple then moved into a $10 million estate in Bedford, New York. She was just 23 years old.

A year later, she told *Ebony* that she was enjoying her life. "It feels good being married, but I never thought I'd be married. I never thought I would because my parents got divorced, and it gives you a different attitude about that type of thing. It kind of hardens you."

Carey explained that she wasn't looking for romance when she began working with Mottola on the album. "We had a lot in common, and we just gradually came together. We don't look at each other as two people with a big age difference. We are just right for each other and that is all that matters. If you are really right for each other, that will shine through all the differences; everything—race and age."

Carey's wedding was a lavish event. Her Vera Wang dress cost $25,000 and had such a long train that it took six people to fold it into the limo.

And, she added, "He's an incredible cook. He's so spoiled me with his food that I can't go to restaurants anymore."

More than anything, Carey told writer Lynn Norment, she was grateful. "I'm really fortunate, I'm really happy, and I'm really lucky to be where I am. All I can do now is be the best I can be."

For a while, it seemed as if Mariah were unstoppable. Her third album, *Music Box*, became her most successful to date. Her 1994 Christmas album spawned a rare new Christmas hit, "All I Want for Christmas Is You," which has become a holiday standard. A year later she released *Daydream*, and the first single, "Fantasy," became only the second record in history to debut at number one on the U.S. charts.

By the mid-1990s, she was one of the most popular and most successful recording artists on the planet. She was possibly one of the most depressed as well.

Behind the image she projected publicly, Carey was miserable. Her marriage had turned into an emotional prison. "People think I've had this fairy-tale life," she said in *Essence*, "that I met this rich prince who gave me a life in the lap of luxury, put me in a mansion, made me a star. It wasn't that way. In fact, it almost killed me."

Mariah says that in the beginning, the relationship was good for her. "Tommy represented something I'd never had — stability. There was mutual respect and his passion for me and my music."

What people didn't realize, she complained, was that she made sure she was always an equal partner, insisting on paying half the bills — from utilities to major house

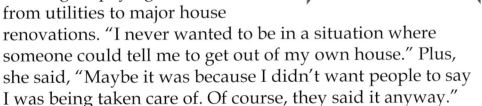

By the mid-1990s, she was one of the most popular and most successful recording artists on the planet.

renovations. "I never wanted to be in a situation where someone could tell me to get out of my own house." Plus, she said, "Maybe it was because I didn't want people to say I was being taken care of. Of course, they said it anyway."

As she got older and more sure of herself and who she was, Mariah and her husband clashed over everything from what she should wear to her hairstyle to what songs she should sing. She felt he wanted to control every aspect of her life.

"I was in a beautiful house surrounded by beautiful things," she told writer Joan Morgan, "but I couldn't be who I really was."

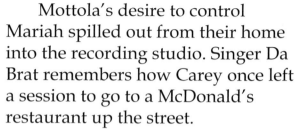

Eventually, Carey realized that all the success in the world meant very little if she was miserable.

Mottola's desire to control Mariah spilled out from their home into the recording studio. Singer Da Brat remembers how Carey once left a session to go to a McDonald's restaurant up the street.

"Two seconds after we left, Tommy was calling the car phone, telling us to come back. They were tripping out that we were going five minutes away to get a cheeseburger. It was like she was on . . . [an] army base."

Mariah began referring to their mansion as Sing Sing, the name of a famous prison.

"There were moments when I thought I was going to die in this relationship," Carey admitted in *Essence*. "I figured I'd been given all the things I'd ever prayed for, so why should I expect to be happy in my personal life? I didn't feel worthy of happiness."

Eventually, Carey realized that all the success in the world meant very little if she was miserable. While she may have had financial security, she had lost herself. With the help of friends like Da Brat and others, she realized that it was up to her to take her life back—but it wouldn't be without a struggle.

As her marriage started to crumble, Mariah confided to her friend Da Brat, *pictured above*, how miserable she was. Carey felt smothered by Mottola, who seemed to want to control everything she did. Finally, after four years of marriage, Mariah filed for divorce.

CHAPTER 5

A Long Climb
Back to the Top

*C*arey divorced Mottola in 1998 but stayed with Sony, the record label he still ran. It was a decision she later came to regret. In April 2001, Mariah left Sony and signed the ill-fated deal with EMI Virgin records.

During an MTV interview promoting her upcoming *Glitter* album, Carey was asked why she felt the need to work to the point of exhaustion. "I think one of the reasons I stay grounded and stay hungry is because I didn't get to experience my fame when it first happened as a young kid just starting out.

"I didn't trust enough to be myself because I was scared. I feel people played on those fears and insecurities. I was shrouded and hidden away, therefore I'm just experiencing this . . . for the first time."

After the dismal showing of *Glitter*, EMI's executives decided to cut their losses and parted ways with the singer. That year, Mariah also buried her father after he died of cancer.

"That put things into perspective," Mariah admitted in *USA Today*. "Sometimes you have to go through difficult stuff, either to learn a lesson or maybe reconnect with something that has slipped away a bit. But that's how life is. You may keep getting hit, but you have to just keep on standing up again."

Carey says her father's death and her career failures made her a better person and a better musical artist.

"It forced me to put the brakes on everything and admit my life wasn't working," she told *Essence*. "I had to reevaluate myself and get re-centered. I discovered that my desire to make music came from the need to heal myself. My desire to become famous came from the need to feel worthy and accepted. And that made me more of a freak than I ever was."

After her hospitalization, Carey began seeing a therapist. "He said I had to start setting boundaries in life, to learn how to say *no*," she revealed to writer Elysa Gardner. "It's taken some people a while to understand that, but now they do. . . . For so long, I had been so busy taking care of everyone and everything else, including my career, that I forgot about me."

The result was the biggest triumph of her career. In May 2002, she signed with Island Records, determined to make the music that she wanted to make—not do songs others thought she should.

> "Sometimes you have to go through difficult stuff, either to learn a lesson or maybe reconnect with something that has slipped away."

"I realized I have to go with my gut," she explained to Jennifer Vineyard. "Because everybody's got an opinion and so many people's opinions about me are polar opposites. So stay in your lane, I'll figure it out." The result was her ninth studio album, *The Emancipation of Mimi*. "I felt I did the album I wanted to do."

After years of personal and professional struggles, Carey found herself back on top with Emancipation of Mimi. *The title refers to Mariah's childhood nickname, Mimi. By November 2005, the record had sold over 7 million copies worldwide. It earned Carey her first Grammys in 15 years.*

Unlike her earlier albums, *The Emancipation of Mimi* is much less reliant on pop vocals. Instead, there is a greater emphasis on R&B, hip-hop and funk. Carey's close friend, rap singer Da Brat, told *Essence*, "Hip-hop is in her bones, in her soul. That child is Black. That girl is ghetto. I know she has always wanted rap in her music. Once she started having more say, she made it happen," collaborating with artists such as Kanye West, Jermaine Dupri, and Snoop Dogg.

The album title refers to the childhood nickname she is still called by her friends and family. Released in 2005, the album would mark a triumphant comeback for Carey, earning her her first Grammys since 1991. The song "We Belong Together" was the most successful of her career, staying at number one for 14 weeks, and was named the *world's* most-played single of 2005.

Against long odds, Mariah was back on top. Da Brat told *Essence* that this time around, Carey has been enjoying the view.

"She can do whatever she wants, she can date whomever she wants, she can say what she wants—she makes her own decisions. . . . She's happy and content and making the music she wants."

The Emancipation of Mimi was 2005's best-selling album and was certified six times platinum in the United States. Carey now had 17 number-one singles, tying her with Elvis for the most number ones by an individual performer. Only

> **The Emancipation of Mimi is much less reliant on pop vocals. Instead, there is emphasis on R&B, hip-hop and funk.**

In February 2006, Mariah won Grammys for Best Female R&B Vocal Performance, Best Contemporary R&B Album, and Best R&B Song from her album Emancipation of Mimi.

the Beatles have more with 21. When she turned 36 in March 2006, some believed she would break the Beatle's longstanding record by the time she turned 40.

Just the thought humbles her. "I don't even want to think about that," she told Rory Evans. "The Beatles are history. So is Elvis. Even if I did break those records, I'm a woman and they're men, so it would be apples and oranges.

"What matters is, I am blessed with a gift to make music."

And she plans to keep making it for a long time to come.

CHRONOLOGY

1970   Born in Long Island on March 27

1972   Parents separate

1986   Records first professional demo

1987   Graduates from Harborfields High School

1988   Begins singing backup for Brenda K. Starr; signs recording contract with Columbia Records

1990   First album, *Mariah Carey*, is released

1991   Wins Best New Artist and Best Pop Vocal Performance Grammys in February

1993   Marries Tommy Mottola on June 5

1997   Separates from Mottola; appears on *MTV Unplugged*

1998   Divorce from Mottola becomes final; begins three-year relationship with singer Luis Miguel

2001   Signs $80 million record deal in April with EMI Virgin; is hospitalized for emotional and physical exhaustion in August

2002   Is dropped by EMI Virgin Records in January; father dies; signs with Island Records

2005   *The Emancipation of Mimi* becomes Carey's comeback album

2006   Carey wins three Grammys in February; begins Adventures of Mimi tour

DISCOGRAPHY

1990	*Mariah Carey*	1998	*#1's*
1991	*Emotions*	1999	*Rainbow*
1992	*MTV Unplugged*	2001	*Glitter*
1993	*Music Box*	2001	*Greatest Hits*
1994	*Merry Christmas*	2002	*Charmbracelet*
1995	*Daydream*	2003	*The Remixes*
1997	*Butterfly*	2005	*The Emancipation of Mimi*

FURTHER READING

Books

Nickson, Chris. *Mariah Carey Revisited: The Unauthorized Biography.* New York: St. Martin's Griffin, 1998.

Parker, Judith. *Mariah Carey.* Danbury, Connecticut: Children's Press, 2001.

Works Consulted

Anderman, Joan. "For Carey, the Glory's Gone But the Glitter Lives On." *Boston Globe,* pg. D.4, September 10, 2003

Armstrong, Mike. "Mariah 'Under Psychiatric Care.'" *E! Online,* August 1, 2001, http://www.eonline.com/News/Items/0,1,8612,00.html

Associated Press. "Carey Turns to 'American Idol' Judge to Help
   Spice Up Summer Tour." May 25, 2006,
   http://www.usatoday.com/life/people/2006-05-25-randy-
   jackson_x.htm?POE=LIFISVA

Associated Press. "Mariah Carey Ties Elvis on Singles Chart."
   December 24, 2005, http://abcnews.go.com/Entertainment/
   wireStory?id=1439334

Kaufman, Gil, and Matt Anderson. "Mariah Carey: Under
   Pressure." VH-1 Interviews, June 19, 2002, http://
   www.vh1.com/artists/interview/1455306/06192002/
   carey_mariah.jhtml

"Mariah Carey." *Blender,* http://www.blender.com/guide/
   artist.aspx?id=600

"Mariah Carey Announces Summer Tour." *Spin.com,* May 22, 2006,
   http://www.spin.com/features/news/2006/05/
   060522_mariah/

"Mariah Carey: 'I'm Not Whacko.'" *CNN,* December 20, 2002,
   http://archives.cnn.com/2002/SHOWBIZ/Music/12/18/
   carey.lkl/index.html

Morgan, Joan. "Mariah Carey: Free at Last." Essence, n.d.
   http://www.essence.com/essence/themix/entertainment/
   0,16109,1037097,00.html

MTV.com. "Mariah Carey."
   http://www.mtv.com/music/artist/carey_mariah/
   artist.jhtml#/music/artist/carey_mariah/artist.jhtml

Norment, Lynn. "Mariah Carey: 'Not Another White Girl Trying to
   Sing Black.'" *Ebony,* March 1991.
——— . "Mariah Carey: Singer Talks About Storybook Marriage,
   Interracial Heritage and Sudden Fame." *Ebony,* April 1994.

Sicha, Choire. "All About Mimi." *Marie Claire,* July 2006,
   http://www.marieclaire.co.uk/celebrity/
   Mariah_Carey_article_85581.html

On the Internet

Mariah Carey Official Web Site
   http://www.mariahcarey.com

The Mariah Carey Archives
   http://www.mcarchives.com

INDEX